1. Introducing Hamsters

Although most people know of the cute little golden or Syrian hamster, few realize that it is actually one of the newer pets when compared with dogs, cats, rabbits, goldfish or even budgerigars and canaries. Further, you might be surprised to learn that all pet hamsters in the world, of this species, can be traced back to just two females and one male that were captured in Aleppo, Syria during 1930.

They were sent to Jerusalem where they bred to form a large nucleus of stock. Some of this was sent to England and elsewhere. Stock at London Zoo became available to the public and from it the hamster fancy began in earnest. Stock arrived in the USA about 1945, so it was only after World War II that the hamster really began to take off as a popular pet.

The number of hamsters kept reaching greater numbers, so mutations began to appear; these were selectively improved by breeders. Today there are about 40 varieties of hamster and these are seen in a wide range of coat colors and patterns. There are also a few interesting fur types to choose from.

The hamster, having only a tiny tail, is often more acceptable to a child's mother than are other small rodents, such as mice or gerbils, and this has no doubt helped it to retain its high level of popularity. It is also a very cuddly little critter which has a large adult following of breeders and exhibitors. The golden hamster has the scientific name of

▶ All hamsters kept in captivity originated from 3 found in Syria in 1930. This is a new variety often referred to as a *saddleback*.

◀ Since hamsters from Syria became so popular, hamsters from China, like this one, have captured our imagination, too.

Hamsters should NOT be given as a gift unless you are certain that the recipient will properly care for the animal.
◄

1

Chinese hamsters, *Cricetus griseus,* are more often called *dwarf hamsters* because they are smaller than the Syrian hamsters. They have not as yet been developed with long hair types and color variations.

Rats, mice and gerbils have long tails which many parents feel is objectionable...that's why hamsters are preferred.

This is the Russian hamster, *Phodopus sungoris.* It, too, is smaller than the Syrian hamster *Mesocricetus auratus.*

Mesocricetus auratus and is a member of the enormous order of animals known as Rodentia—the rodents. These are all characterized by having two pairs of gnawing incisor teeth. There are in fact quite a number of wild hamsters and in recent years two of these, the Chinese *(Cricetus griseus)* and the Russian *(Phodopus sungoris)* have also started to become popular.

Hamsters are not long lived, an average being about two years of age, so it is important that you obtain youngsters. They are weaned from their mother's milk by the time they are just three weeks old, so anytime after this is the time to obtain them. It is best to keep these pets as individuals because once sexually mature, at about six weeks of age, the females, which are larger than the males, will often attack them. Males will also fight each other. Sometimes pairs that are brought up together from babies will live happily together, but don't count on this.

If you wish to enjoy your hamster to the fullest, be sure you handle it carefully, and often, from a

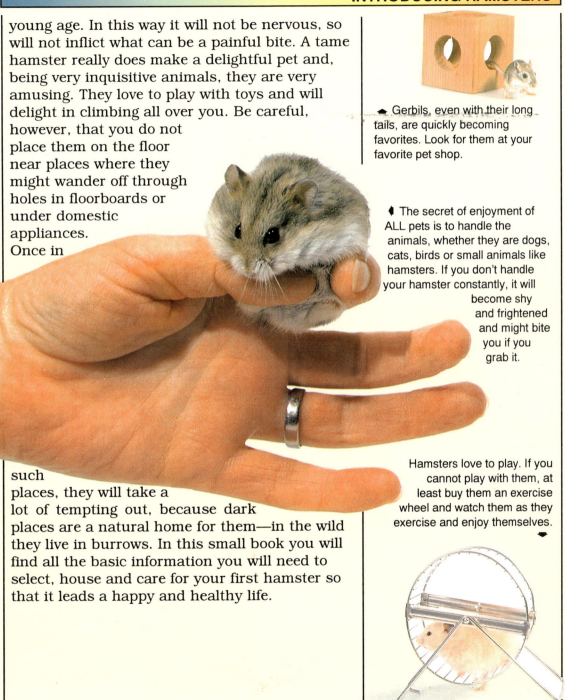

young age. In this way it will not be nervous, so will not inflict what can be a painful bite. A tame hamster really does make a delightful pet and, being very inquisitive animals, they are very amusing. They love to play with toys and will delight in climbing all over you. Be careful, however, that you do not place them on the floor near places where they might wander off through holes in floorboards or under domestic appliances. Once in

▲ Gerbils, even with their long tails, are quickly becoming favorites. Look for them at your favorite pet shop.

◀ The secret of enjoyment of ALL pets is to handle the animals, whether they are dogs, cats, birds or small animals like hamsters. If you don't handle your hamster constantly, it will become shy and frightened and might bite you if you grab it.

such places, they will take a lot of tempting out, because dark places are a natural home for them—in the wild they live in burrows. In this small book you will find all the basic information you will need to select, house and care for your first hamster so that it leads a happy and healthy life.

Hamsters love to play. If you cannot play with them, at least buy them an exercise wheel and watch them as they exercise and enjoy themselves. ◆

← Your pet shop will have many hamster cages. As with all things, it is a matter of taste and finances which eventually determine which cage you buy. Keep in mind that the cage must be cleaned (emptied) periodically.

🖐 Cages are not only to keep the hamsters IN. They are also to keep predators (like dogs, cats and snakes) OUT. Hamsters can escape from the smallest hole, so be careful. Hamsters that escape almost always die.

A hamster needs a minimum of 18 x 12 inches...larger is better. The bottom should be covered with suitable odor-absorbing material such as those recommended on page 9. ←

2. Accommodation

The housing needs of a hamster can be satisfied in one of three ways. A plastic or glass aquarium with a weldwire mesh fitted on to it makes an excellent home, as do any of the large hamster cages available from all good pet shops. There is also an interesting housing system produced that was designed to mimic the natural home of these pets. We will look at each in turn.

The Aquarium Home

An aquarium has the advantage that it is easy to see into, can be as spacious as your money will allow you to

spend on it, and is hygienic, being easy to clean. The glass unit will not scratch like the molded plexiglas ones, but it will be more expensive to purchase. The minimum size should be 45x30cm (18x12in) and there is no upper limit because as with any pet's housing it can never be too big. In order to secure the top you can place a weldwire lid onto it and hold it in place with a heavy weight, or any other means.

It will require a small sleeping box placed in it and this can be made of plastic or of plywood. This will need a small entrance hole

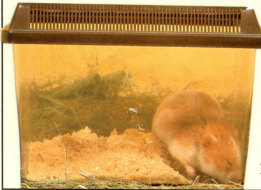

◄ An old aquarium, even if it leaks or has a small crack, is usually suitable as a home for your hamster. You must be certain, however, that the top is VERY securely attached so the hamster cannot escape.

New aquariums are inexpensive enough for hamster homes.

in it, and a hinged lid if you like so you can open it up as needed. Other fittings are discussed later.

The Commercial Hamster Cage

There are numerous cages made for hamsters, some being altogether better than others. Choose the largest you can afford. Those with deep plastic bases are better than those made of metal. The latter eventually start to rust due to the hamster's urine seeping through the floor covering. Check that there are no protruding pieces of metal on the cage bars as these might injure your pet. This type of cage has a chrome type canopy of bars and these clip onto the base. See that they create a snug fit because hamsters are masters of escaping through comparatively small openings.

Commercial units usually come with a wheel and a small sleeping box; the better ones also have a raised platform and a ladder.

Susan and Stephanie have the ultimate hamster cage. It is fully equipped with everything that a hamster could want! ►

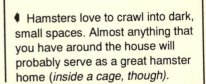

◄ Hamsters love to crawl into dark, small spaces. Almost anything that you have around the house will probably serve as a great hamster home (*inside a cage, though*).

◄ The most popular of hamster homes is the wonderful *Hagen Habitrail* which has an enormous number of variations possible with add-ons. Your local pet shop should be able to show you the latest in *HABITRAIL* formations.

Very inexpensive *Small Pal Pens* are also available at your local pet shop. They serve hamsters well since hamsters must be kept isolated once they have grown up. ►

Tube Housing Systems

This accommodation is comprised of a basic kit which can be added to in order to make it larger and larger. The base unit is a circular plastic tub from which a plastic tube leads up into another tub. One provides a small living area and the other is a 'bedroom'. The basic kit does not provide over-generous quarters but with additional tubes and tubs you can make a fascinating home network that gives the hamster plenty of exercise as it moves from one room to another. The idea of the system is to recreate the tunnels and compartments found in the burrows of the wild hamster. It is one of the few commercial units that have been designed to provide a small pet with some semblance of its natural home.

Cage Furnishings

Whatever house you provide for your hamster you should supply it with a number of essential or useful furnishings. It will need a small crock (earthenware) feeding dish. These are much better than dishes made in plastic, which easily tip over. A hamster drinking bottle is preferred to an open dish. The bottle is inverted and from it a tube extends and has a ball bearing in its end. As the hamster licks at the bearing this is raised and so water is dispensed. It is clean and keeps the water fresher than an open container, which soon

These Chinese hamsters are having a lot of fun with these plastic tubes. All hamsters should have toys with which they exercise.

The hamster drinking bottle only offers water when the end is licked.

Pet shops offer Hagen Hamster Starter Kits which contain everything you need to start right.

becomes dirtied with sawdust or other floor coverings.

An exercise wheel will be appreciated by a hamster and it will spend much time in it. Those with solid floors are superior to those which are all wire. All small rodents enjoy scampering through tubes. These can be suitably sized pieces of plastic or they can be made of cardboard. A few stout twigs will also be a source of

Every cage should have a proper feeding dish. Crockery is preferred.

Alfalfa can serve as a food item as well as a bedding material and nest liner. Photo courtesy of Hagen.

This long haired (Angora) grey hamster likes to sleep in a child's purse.

Hamsters like toys in which they can hide. It gives them a feeling of security.

It's not a good idea to keep two hamsters together, as they will likely fight.

Be sure that any vegetation that is offered to your hamster has not been chemically treated.

This hamster cage is poorly constructed because the wires should have been horizontal rather than vertical to allow the hamster exercising possibilities.

Hamster toys often can be linked together to make long tunnels or labyrinths.

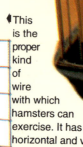

This is the proper kind of wire with which hamsters can exercise. It has both horizontal and vertical spacings.

curiosity to a hamster, and it will nibble away on this as it will on used wooden cotton reels. If space permits you can include a rock or two in order to create a more interesting landscape than just a plain floor.

Floor and Sleeping Area Coverings

For the living area you can use sawdust as it is highly absorbent. You could add a top layer of wood shavings if required. For the sleeping area the choice is hay, proprietary fiber made for hamsters, mice and gerbils, or shredded paper. Meadow hay is a good choice because it contains various dried wild plants which the hamster will nibble on. Granulated paper is the latest form of covering for the living area.

Place a generous layer of material on the floor so it absorbs any liquid, such as juices from fruits, and of course urine. Place enough bedding material in the sleeping compartment so the hamster can make a cozy nest. The cage should be cleaned on a very regular basis to prevent it from smelling, but mainly to minimize the risk of bacterial build up. This chore should be attended to every week at the very least.

◄ The bottom of your hamster cage MUST be covered with absorbent material. This material should be changed regularly.

This hamster cage is not large enough for three hamsters! Territorial disputes might result from keeping three females together.
▶

◄ Pet shops stock many kinds of absorbent materials that can be used to line the cage tray. Photo courtesy of Hagen.

◆ When choosing a hamster, select an active one, not a passive animal that sits with its eyes closed.

If you want Chinese Dwarf hamsters, you can select a male by his extended, rounded rump (last hamster, far right); the female, center, has teats and a more **V**-pointed rump. ◆

3. Choosing a Hamster

Three factors are important when you are selecting a hamster. Firstly, it should be young, secondly very healthy, and finally of a variety you find appealing. The sex is not important in a pet as both will make delightful little companions for you. If you are planning to breed then of course you will want one of each sex, and you will ideally prefer a quality pair of a known variety. It is, after all, as inexpensive to breed quality hamsters

Look closely at the hamster's eyes. Stay away from half-closed, weepy eyes. The coat should be dry and not matted.

as it is those of unknown ancestry.

Age

If the hamster is to be a pet, then the younger the better. This so, one which is about four weeks old is ideal. At this age it will be independent of its mother and eating well. It will also be very receptive to being handled. If you plan to breed straight away, then choose

A good way to ascertain whether a hamster is young or old is to take the smallest animal you can find at the pet shop.

one which is about three months of age or a little older. It will be physically better able to do this than the young sexually mature but physically underdeveloped animal. If the hamsters you see are large and housed in individual cages, the chances are they are fully mature—and will be difficult to assess in terms of their age. They may not have too long to live!

Health

The first thing you should look at when obtaining a hamster is not the animal but its accommodation. This should be very clean, free

← Healthy hamsters have healthy appetites. If your hamster stops eating, find out why.

from odor, and not be cramped, damp or overcrowded with stock. If any of these conditions are seen then it is best to seek another source of supply.

You should watch the hamsters in their cage before actually inspecting any. Often they are asleep in a heap; but if some are on the move, check that they are walking with no signs of a problem, such as being all hunched up with the

← A hand-tamed hamster is worth more than a wild one. Ask your pet shop operator if he sells hand-tamed animals.

A healthy Syrian hamster...it looks healthy!

← Active hamsters, like this dark chocolate animal, are usually healthy. When a hamster is ill, it usually becomes lethargic.

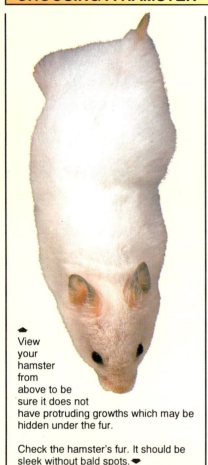

View your hamster from above to be sure it does not have protruding growths which may be hidden under the fur.

Check the hamster's fur. It should be sleek without bald spots.

fur standing away from its lie. Select one or two for close scrutiny. The eyes should be round and clear with no signs of weeping or staining around them. The nose should be dry and not swollen or discharging any liquid. Inspect the teeth to see they are neatly aligned, the top ones just overlapping but touching those of the lower jaw.

A hamster's ears should be erect and not held back at an angle to the head.

Rodents gnaw a great deal and to compensate for the wearing process the teeth grow continually. If they are not correctly aligned they will grow up or down as the case may be and will penetrate the jaw. They will then not be able to eat properly. The condition is known as malocclusion, and whilst a vet can trim overgrown incisor teeth, such animals are of no use for breeding and hardly suited as new pets.

The fur of the hamster should be sleek (for most varieties) and regardless of variety there should be no bald areas or any signs of abrasions to the skin. Look carefully for any indication of skin parasites, usually lice or mites rather than fleas. Any dry scabby areas of skin might indicate ringworm, a fungal infection that is extremely difficult to cure. Inspect the anal region carefully because hamsters suffer from a condition known as 'wet tail' which is a disease of the digestive tract that manifests itself in the tail region becoming wet. A hamster with this problem is not long for this world—maybe seven days. Check the abdomen of the youngster for any signs of swelling—which applies to any part of its body. See that the legs and feet are free from any damage.

If all looks well, and the others you have selected to inspect also look well, then pick out the one you want. Unless you are unfortunate, it should prove a healthy little pet. If any of those you look at show signs of an illness, then I would reject any from that establishment because there is a good chance the others will have contracted the problem, which has not yet shown itself. Small animals, such as hamsters, are not easily cured once they become ill so why take chances?

An active Chinese Dwarf hamster climbing a ladder. Usually if a hamster climbs it cannot be seriously ill.

Hamsters can be brushed with an old, soft toothbrush. Usually, though, hamsters keep themselves well groomed.

This hamster likes to push this crystal dinner bell. The sounds it produces seems to entertain him.

Hamsters like to climb, but their feet are delicate, so sharp wires should NOT be offered as they will climb them even if they are dangerous to their feet.

CONTAINS AIR BARRIER BAG
Maintains optimal vitamin potency
NET. WT. 4¼ OZ.

ART. # H-1012

➤ In addition to its basic diet, your hamster will appreciate treat foods, which are tasty as well as nutritious. Photo courtesy of Hagen.

4. Feeding

The hamster, like all rodents, is very cosmopolitan in its dietary needs. It is a herbivore, which means it will eat virtually anything of a vegetative origin. In order to ensure it lacks no essential vitamins or minerals in its diet, it is best to provide a wide-ranging menu. Although a herbivore, it does enjoy certain foods of animal origin, so milk, cheese, eggs and bread soaked in beef extracts are all taken to a greater or lesser degree and provide a rich source of protein, which is important to these particular pets.

The basic diet will be composed of various cereal crops, seeds, fruits and vegetables—the animal-origin foods being supplemental. You can purchase cartons of premixed hamster foods from your pet store. These foods are scientifically formulated to provide optimum nourishment to your pet. They're economical, too, so it won't pay you to scrimp on your pet's diet by offering surplus foods from your kitchen.

Cereal Crops & Seeds

Crushed or dehusked oats (groats), rather than whole oats, are a basic ingredient of hamster mixes. Whole oats are rather hard and difficult for a hamster to cope with—the sharp husks might also create abrasions. Flaked corn is another popular cereal crop, along with maize, wheat, barley and bran. Cornflakes and

Art. # 61048   Art. # 61050   Art. # 61052   Art. # 61056   Art. # 61058   Art. # 61060

◀ Living World Habitrail is a line of best-selling foods and supplements for hamsters. The Habitrail is the expandable hamster palace (see page 6).

other breakfast cereals can by all means be included into the mix. All of these are rich in carbohydrates and are thus basic energy foods.

Various seeds will be eagerly taken and these include unsalted peanuts, sunflower, millets and canary seed. The first two named are very rich in proteins and, especially, fats, so ration these. Otherwise, your hamster might start to get rather portly! You can include most nuts,

All species of hamsters require clean, fresh food which is varied as much as possible.

Hamsters store food in their cheek pouches only to facilitate moving it from where they find it to where they will store it.

◀ Hamsters use their hands to hold their food when it is too large to take into their mouth in its entirety. Most rodents, even squirrels, do this...but not dogs or cats!

Sunflower seeds are eaten with relish but they do not have enough vitamins, minerals and other basic requirements to be used as the sole diet for hamsters. ◀

though large ones should be broken up into more manageable pieces.

Fruits and Vegetables

The list of possibilities here is almost unlimited, so you can work on the basis that if you can eat it, so can your hamster. Apples in particular seem to be a favored and useful fruit to include. Try your pet on a whole range of fruit and veggies to see

which it likes best. Under this heading can be included hay, wild plants such as clover, chickweed and others, as well as flowering plants. Avoid buttercups and others known to be poisonous, which includes any plants grown from bulbs. Be sure that any wild plants gathered in the country are not picked from verges which may have been contaminated by exhaust fumes or by dogs. If taken from

◄These Chinese Dwarf hamsters have been offered a good mix of seeds and prepared staple food.

Hamsters, like this black hamster, enjoy pieces of apple and other fresh fruits. ◄

If you get very friendly with your hamster, you can train him to BEG for food. ◄

A hamster has the ability and dentition to open this walnut and eat the walnut meat. ◄

your garden, be sure the plants have not been subject to being sprayed with chemicals. It is wise to rinse greenfoods first.

Pellets prepared for rabbits will be enjoyed by the hamster, but use these sparingly as they are very concentrated. Laboratories use these almost exclusively to feed their stock, but they must become a very boring diet to the hamsters, so you are better to use them purely as a supplement to fresh foods.

Your pet will enjoy dog biscuits, cookies, and cake but try to avoid feeding too many sweet items as these are no more beneficial to hammy than they are to you and me. You can obtain various multivitamin powders which are dusted onto fruits, so they will adhere to these, but the use of such products has no benefit, quite the reverse, if you are already feeding a well balanced and varied diet.

Water

Although wild hamsters live in an area that is largely desert, they nonetheless need a constant supply of water at their disposal. This should be fresh daily. If their diet is more dry than wet they will consume more water than if it is the reverse.

Feeding Schedule

It is best to adopt a regular timetable for feeding your hamster and in this way it will come to look forward to its next meal to see what is on offer. Give it fresh fruits, greens

← A hamster should never have access to houseplants, as many of them are poisonous.

← Large nuts are great toy foods, but they take too long to be eaten. Offer a few large nuts weekly so the hamster can wear down his ever-growing teeth

← Hamsters...like puppies...need to chew. If you don't offer him something healthy upon which to chew, he'll chew on the first piece of wood that he finds.

◀ This Chinese Dwarf hamster has his whole meal in his feeding dish. If you see what he eats first, you'll learn what his favorite foods are.

etc., in the morning, and remove any uneaten by the next meal in the late afternoon. This meal can be composed of dry foods and any supplementary tidbits.

Hamsters store much of their food, which is gathered in pouches on either side of their jaws. They will take it to their nest to nibble on it as they feel the need. Often they will also store it somewhere and then forget it, so always be on the lookout for such caches so these do not start to decay and attract pathogenic bacteria. Remember to store all food items in cool darkened places so they will stay fresher longer, and never feed any items that you are doubtful about in terms of their freshness.

◄ Your hamster will only be as healthy as the food it eats. Hamster feed is NOT very expensive.

◄ Pet shops carry name brands of fresh hamster food. DO NOT pour the feed onto the bottom of the cage!! Put it into the food dish.

Coprophagy (Refection)
This term is used to describe the

◄ This can be the morning meal for your hamster...fresh vegetables which you yourself eat. Remove what remains after 4 hours or so.

process whereby certain mammals, such as rodents, rabbits and hares, eat food which has passed through their digestive system without being fully utilized. It forms small pellets that are passed out of the body via the anus. To the person not aware of this it can look as though the animal is eating its own fecal matter, but this is not the case, the two types of pellet being totally different. The food pellets, after being swallowed, pass through the digestive system a second time where gut bacteria are able to act on them a second time—more fully. This need arises because the cellulose walls of plant matter are very strong and not effectively broken down the first time through the system.

A lovely cream hamster and his fresh seed lunch.

→ Special chews may be hung inside the cage. Be sure that the chew is designed for hamsters and not for birds. Wires inside the chew usually don't bother birds but they might well make a hamster ill.

→ Enjolic Smith wants a hamster as a pet...but she must FIRST learn how to care for it. Hopefully she will read this book (or any of the other hamster books available at pet shops), BEFORE she gets her hamster.

5. Breeding

Before you decide to become a breeder of hamsters, it is prudent to consider the following. There are many commercial breeding farms that produce thousands of hamsters every year. They can sell them at prices far cheaper than you can. The result is that pet shops are never short on supplies, so if you breed hamsters you must consider how you will dispose of the surplus stock you will quickly have left. Further, after just a few weeks the stock must be housed in its own accommodation. Otherwise, the youngsters will soon be fighting each other.

Pet stores have many toys for hamsters. This female used this toy house as her nursery!

The answer is to be sure you commence in only a very low key manner. If you are wise you will also only breed quality stock of varieties that your local pet stores find popular. In this way you may have an advantage over the commercial farms, which are more concerned with quantity rather than quality. Further, if you also exhibit your best stock, you will

When a female becomes pregnant, she grows larger and larger until she has her babies. Hamsters can reproduce when only six weeks old.

build up a reputation for this and will meet potential buyers at the shows.

Given these facts, then the best way to commence breeding is to make contact with a reputable breeder in your area that maybe specializes in the variety you like best. It is important you know the genotype of your foundation stock from the outset. Just buying any old stock may produce some cute little hamsters but these will not breed true and so you will end up with the very hamsters that have the lowest value.

Sexing

If you inspect the underside of a young hamster you will find two basic differences between the sexes. Firstly, the female has, normally, 14 teats, the male has none. You will have to part the fur carefully to see these. Secondly, the anal—genital distance is greater in the male than in the female. Further, with a mature hamster the male has a more bulbous anal tail region when viewed from the side—however, this is not always a totally reliable guide.

◆ Hamsters are not difficult to sex if you can handle them or watch them climb a ladder. This is an immature female as evidenced by her teats.

This lovely hamster, sometimes called an OB (for orange-blotched), is a male. His bulky rump is a dead giveaway.
◆

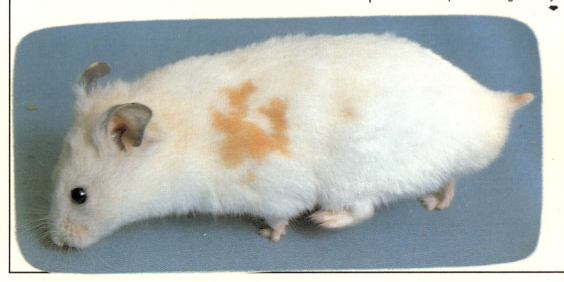

← Hamsters mating. The male is always atop the female. Females are usually much larger than males.

Breeding Facts

Hamsters are sexually mature by the age of about six weeks but it is best not to breed from them until they are about twelve weeks old when they will be more physically mature. The female estrus cycles every four days and once mated the gestation period is a rapid sixteen days. The babies are born blind and helpless but develop very rapidly. Within a few days they will be nibbling at hard foods and by the age of about 3-4 weeks will be fully independent of their mother, and should be removed from her lest she attacks them.

Mating Procedure

The female is larger than the male and will not hesitate to attack him if she is not ready to mate. When you wish to pair your hamsters you should always place the female in the male's quarters, never the other way around. This applies to most

♦This is a six-week-old female ready for breeding. It is best to wait another few weeks before mating her. Females which are not ready for mating can inflict serious injury on a smaller, aggressive male.

animals. Alternatively, you can use breeding cages which are small and have a central dividing partition such that the two can see each other. The male is placed in first and when he has settled down the female is introduced, either into his quarters or into the breeding unit. In the latter case if the two seem very interested in each other you can remove the partition.

In the former case the two will sniff each other a while and either mating will take place, or the female will attack her prospective partner. If this

◗ When you wish to breed your hamsters, place the female into the male's cage. Be sure they have areas to keep themselves separate from one another.

Two fancy varieties of Syrian hamster breeding. Pairing such different colors usually results in poor quality offspring. As an amateur breeder, you should ONLY breed the best. The BEST is what your local pet shop will buy from you. ☚

This nest contains eleven baby hamsters only six days old. They were buried in the nesting material which was removed to facilitate this photo.

The same nest as above when the babies are two weeks old. They are already fully marked but their eyes are still closed. They can be kept with their mother until they are about four weeks of age, after which they must be removed or they might be attacked by their mother.

A very suitable nest was found by this mother hamster. She found a coil of hemp rope and used it successfully for a month during which she raised 8 babies.

happens remove her and try again a day or two later until a mating transpires. Once mated, the female can be returned to her own quarters where she will have her litter.

The Birth

You must be very gentle in handling the pregnant hamster. As it gets within a day or two of the birth it is best to leave her alone. She will produce 6-9 babies and potentially as many as 16. During the prenatal weeks she should be given items such as bread and milk so that she obtains the needed extra calcium and protein—eggs and cheese at this time will also ensure a good protein intake.

Do not keep a breeding female on a wire base as this not only increases the risk of her killing her babies, but it also denies her the opportunity to practice refection. This is true of any hamster and I do not like wire floors for any form of livestock. The mother hamster having her first litter becomes very nervous and more than a few will kill their babies as a protection if they feel stressed or threatened. Likewise, an unhealthy or under nourished female is likely to kill the babies.

If you have a hinged lid fitted to the sleeping quarters you can check on the babies whilst the mother is preoccupied with eating tidbits. Avoid handling the

These babies are 15 days old and are just starting to open their eyes.

youngsters until they are well established, otherwise, this might trigger the mother to kill them because of the scent you have left on them. You can always rub your hands in soiled sawdust which will reduce the risk of this if you have a need to pick the babies up.

Record Keeping

Any serious breeder will keep detailed records of all matings and the results of these. These should include data on the parents, how many young were born, how many died, the sex ratios, the colors and markings of the babies as they become clear, and how healthy they were before you sold them. Such records will enable you to back track if problems arise. You will be able to ascertain the virility of the parents, how good the mother is in rearing the kits, and whether the type and color of the stock is improving.

This Chinese Dwarf is only 9 days old.

8. Which Variety?

The hamster ancestors of today's varieties were auburn colored agouti with a cream abdomen. The color was more attractive than most wild agouti colors, both because it was a more pleasing shade and because it carried black 'flashes'. These are bands of black which extend from the front of the shoulder upwards and backwards, to terminate a little distance behind the ears. From this appealing combination all present colors, patterns and coat types have evolved as a result of mutations which have been retained and selectively bred from.

The first mutation was the piebald which appeared in 1947. Thereafter, mutations started to appear every 2-5 years, with those affecting coat type—satin, rex and longhair—happening in the years 1969-72. A mutation, which affects the way a gene expresses itself, can occur at any time and in any person's stock. It can then be transferred to other varieties, and in this way new varieties are developed. Once established, a mutant gene can be improved by selection of modifiers. These are lots of other genes (polygenes) which, on a build up basis, modify the intensity of a major gene's expression. By this method the gorgeous velvet-like texture of the rex rabbit's fur has been developed to an outstanding level. This will happen in the hamster as the years go by, and already you can choose from some super varieties. If you plan to breed specific colors, then you should learn about the way genes act (genetics). This will then enable you to work out what your chances are of obtaining such colors, and which genes would be needed to obtain new colors. Here we can look at a few of the popular colors, patterns and coat types. To see the full range of possibilities you are advised to attend a major

◄ *Top,* The color of a hamster has nothing to do with its friendliness. *Left,* This piebald was supposed to be the beginning of a golden-faced hamster with a white body. It never happened!

hamster exhibition where you can discuss these with specialist breeders.

Cinnamon

This color is created when black is taken from the color of the normal wild type. The result is a very pleasing orange-cinnamon. On many low grade cinnamons you will still see traces of the flashes. The eyes are red, which will get darker with age. The gene responsible for this color is identified as b for brown. Very similar in color is the rust which is somewhat darker in shade. As a result the eyelids are darker, as is the eye color, which is all but black in a mature individual. The identified gene creating this color is r for rust.

Creams

There are numerous cream hamsters and these may have black or red eyes. They range from very light to dark creams, the deeper tones being the preferred exhibition choice. Such exhibits should display a very even shade of color. There are some dark areas on a cream and these will be on the ears and in the eyes; in the red eyed variety they will be light brown. The gene creating cream is identified as e and can be combined with rust or cinnamon to create the various shades of cream.

Albino

A true albino does not exist in the hamster, a situation that applies to other animals, including the horse, but the form can be created by other genetic

This is a cream hamster. There are many colors called *cream*. Some have black eyes and some red eyes. The ears usually have darker fur.

Hamsters are bred for color as well as coat types. This is a banded hamster with a white band around its middle.

◂ This is technically called a *cinnamon dominant spot female* hamster. She has red eyes which indicates she has no melanophores (black pigments) in her coat.

combinations. There is a mutant gene, designated cd, that removes or, more correctly, prevents expression, of any colors that the hamster might be carrying. However, some pigment is still exhibited on the ears—thus it is not a true albino. The eye color is red, this being the hemoglobin of the blood that is seen, not a pigment. There is also a dark-eyed albino.

Black Eyed White

This color is created by the dominant mutational gene Wh which,when combined with the e gene that removes black pigmentation, yields the black eyed

▾ To the left is a grey dominant spot female; to the right is a cinnamon dominant spot female.

white. However, this form is a heterozygote, meaning non purebreeding. If two B.E.whites are paired together they will yield a percentage of youngsters that are born with either no eyes or very small ones, so it is not a favored pairing. The way to avoid such youngsters is to mate the white with a black eyed cream. From such a pairing it is not possible to ever obtain the Wh gene in double quantity, so you will get black eyed creams and whites in various ratios (theoretically 50% of each).

Black

The arrival of the umbrous or sooty mutational gene U has given rise to some interesting colors of which the near black is but one. This is produced by pairing with the black eyed cream. If the resulting offspring are mated to the rust color the result will be chocolate hamsters.

Grays and Similar Shades

The light gray mutation is an attractive hamster and is created by the dominant gene Lg. This is lethal in its double (purebreeding) form, meaning that if paired together, two light grays will produce smaller litters because a percentage (theoretically 25%) of the offspring will die before being born. All light grays are therefore heterozygotes—they carry only one gene for the gray mutation.

The dark gray mutation is more attractive than the light one and is inherited as a normal recessive so there are no problems associated with it. If a dark gray is paired with a cinnamon it will yield lilacs, which are a pale gray with a hint of pink. Dark gray paired to rust will create the dove, similar to the lilac but with black eyes compared to the red of the lilac. The smoke pearl, which is a soft gray variety having dark eyes and ears and pale cheek flashes (the paler the better), is created when the dark gray is paired to a cream.

Other hamster colors include the blondes, caramel, and honey.

A satinized cinnamon female hamster.

Above, A long-haired dark grey male, 2 months old. *Below,* A satinized chocolate-and-white female hamster.

A satinized chocolate-and-white female hamster.

A golden umbrous banded female hamster.

A chocolate roan female hamster.

Coat Patterns

The colors so far described are basically singles but a number of beautiful hamsters have patterned coats.

Tortoiseshell

This is tricolored, having gold, yellow and white in various proportions. This is an interesting variety because the color is sex linked, meaning that tortie and whites are both female and non purebreeding. Any pairing involving this variety will always produce a percentage of normal colored offspring. The best pairing to produce the most torties would be normal x yellow which will theoretically produce 50%. Other matings involving a tortie female will yield only 25% tortie. The tortie gene is designated as To.

Banded

The banded hamster sports a variably sized band of white around its midriff. This is often uneven or in some other way not symmetrical. The latter is the ideal exhibition animal. If the banded gene, which is a dominant designated Ba, is combined with certain other genes for white, the size of the band increases, too much for an exhibition hamster but it does produce some pretty pets.

Piebald and Spotting

These two varieties are visually very similar and also not without their breeding problems. They are created by the mutant genes s and Ds. Both result in variably sized white spotting. This term means areas of white, rather than actual spots. A hamster can thus have a few very small white areas or it could be largely a white individual—just as in any piebald animal (note that piebald in hamsters does not infer black and white as in most species—skewbald might be a more appropriate term). The resulting hamsters can be extremely attractive and the spotting can be combined with any color. On the down side, the piebalds tend to be undersized and lack virility. They can be nervous creatures prone to biting. The dominant spot is far better in these matters but it is a lethal gene so two such hamsters paired together will produce reduced litter size because of prenatal deaths of any offspring having a double dose of the Ds gene. The variety is thus non purebreeding. If two piebalds produce any normal colored offspring this confirms that one of the parents must have been a dominant spot and not a piebald.

A golden umbrous satin Angora hamster.

Coat Types

The satin is the oldest of the hair mutations and results in a high sheen to the fur. The colors in satins appear rather darker than in their normal counterparts. Some satins have rather thin hair and these are undesirable and are created when satins are paired together. The responsible gene is the semi dominant Sa.

The preferred hamster will be a heterozygote Sasa. If you did not wish to have any of the 'ultra satins' the policy would be to always breed satins to non satins of the same color.

The rex mutation appeared a year after the satin, in 1970. Its effect is to reduce the length of the guard

Above, A long-haired, satinized, pale-eared red-eyed white hamster, often called an *albino. Below,* A group of young females, left to right: tortoise shell, white bellied tortoise shell, light grey tortoise shell, and a satinized dominant spot tortoise shell.

▲ A young satinized dominant spot hamster.

hairs to create a velvet like coat and curved facial whiskers. In order to improve the quality of the coat you must only breed from those displaying a full dense coat—and which are also good sized individuals. The rex gene is designated as re.

The longhair or Angora mutation results in a longer coat and in a good example this can be impressive. It is the result of the mutant gene l. In the USA this variety is also referred to as the 'teddy'. It is to be hoped breeders do not take hair length to extremes, as in the Peruvian variety of guinea pigs. The color of Angoras tends to be paler than in their normal counterparts, and the male has the longer coat of the two sexes, due to the presence of sex hormones. The coat mutations can be brought together with each other and with any color and pattern to create an array of differing and interesting forms.

Other Hamsters

At this time the Chinese and Russian hamsters are gaining in popularity. They are both a gray brown agouti color and have a black stripe down their spine. The Russian species displays seasonal coat color changes, becoming paler in the winter.

◀ A fully mature female Angora satinized dominant spot.

◄ A winter white Dwarf Russian hamster.